RHINOCEROS

Jen Green

Grolier
an imprint of

SCHOLASTIC

www.scholastic.com/librarypublishing

Published 2009 by Grolier
An imprint of Scholastic Library Publishing
Old Sherman Turnpike, Danbury,
Connecticut 06816

For The Brown Reference Group plc
Project Editor: Jolyon Goddard
Picture Researcher: Clare Newman
Designers: Dave Allen, Jeni Child, John
Dinsdale, Lynne Ross, Sarah Williams
Managing Editors: Bridget Giles, Tim Harris

Volume ISBN-13: 978-0-7172-8034-6
Volume ISBN-10: 0-7172-8034-9

**Library of Congress
Cataloging-in-Publication Data**

Nature's children. Set 4.
    p. cm.
  Includes bibliographical references and
index.
  ISBN 13: 978-0-7172-8083-4
  ISBN 10: 0-7172-8083-7 ((set 4) : alk. paper)
  1. Animals--Encyclopedias, Juvenile. 1.
Grolier (Firm)
  QL49.N385 2009
  590.3--dc22

                            2007046315

Printed and bound in China

Contents

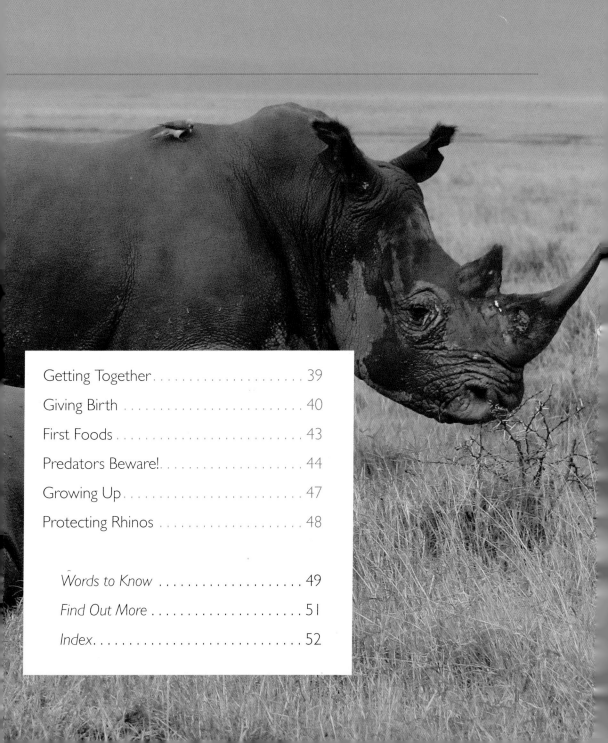

FACT FILE: Rhinoceros

Class	Mammals (Mammalia)
Order	Odd-toed ungulates (Perissodactyla)
Family	Rhinoceros family (Rhinocerotidae)
Genera	*Ceratotherium, Diceros, Dicerorhinus,* and *Rhinoceros*
Species	White rhino (*Ceratotherium simum*), black rhino (*Diceros bicornis*), Sumatran rhino (*Dicerorhinus sumatrensis*), Indian rhino (*Rhinoceros unicornis*), and Javan rhino (*R. sondaicus*)
World distribution	Parts of Africa and southern Asia
Habitat	Varied, including grasslands, scrublands, and forests
Distinctive physical characteristics	Large barrel-shaped body with thick skin; feet have three toes; large head with small eyes and one or two horns on the snout
Habits	Most rhinoceroses are solitary, but white rhinos are more sociable; different species feed by night or day
Diet	Vegetation

Introduction

Which big, bulky **mammal** has one or two horns
on its nose? It's a rhinoceros. These horns are
what make the rhino so easy to recognize.
Rhinos are also easily identified by their long,
barrel-shaped body and sturdy, pillarlike legs.
The big, rectangular head has small eyes and
delicate, leaf-shaped ears. The rhino's thick
skin looks like armor plating.

   Rhinoceroses are the world's second-largest
land mammals, after elephants. They are
surprisingly fast runners and keen swimmers.
Female rhinos make good mothers and are
fiercely protective of their young.

**A mother rhino
keeps a close eye
on her young.**

Rhinos are the heaviest members of the hoofed mammals.

Rhino Relatives

Rhinos are members of the large family of hoofed mammals. This family includes deer, cattle, horses, hippopotamuses, pigs, camels, and giraffes. These hoofed members are divided into two groups—the even-toed group and the odd-toed group.

Rhinos have an odd number of toes—three on each foot. They are, therefore, grouped with horses, which have just one toe on each foot, and tapirs, which have three, like the rhino. However, some scientists suggest that a rhinoceros's closest relatives are elephants, which are not hoofed, and hippos, which have an even number of toes!

Five Types

Rhinoceroses live in parts of Africa and Asia. There are five **species**, or types, of rhinos. They vary in size and shape, and also in the type of place, or habitat, in which they live.

White rhinos are also called square-lipped rhinos. They live on the grassy plains of Africa. Black rhinos also live in Africa. These rhinos can live in a variety of different habitats, from dry scrublands to woodlands and forests.

The other three types of rhinos come from southern Asia. The Sumatran rhino is the smallest type of rhino and it is sometimes hairy. It lives in forests and uplands in Southeast Asia. As its name suggests, the Javan rhino lives on the island of Java in Southeast Asia. It is very rare. Indian rhinos live in grasslands and forests in northeastern India and in nearby Nepal.

The Indian rhinoceros is also called the greater one-horned rhinoceros.

Stocky, columnlike legs support a white rhino's great weight.

Different Sizes

The white rhino is the world's biggest rhinoceros. The only land mammals that are bigger are the African and Asian elephants. At up to 6 feet (1.8 m) high, white rhinos stand taller than most humans. They measure up to 13 feet (4 m) long. They can weigh up to 3½ tons (3.6 tonnes). That's more than three small cars!

At the other end of the scale, the Sumatran rhino is the smallest rhino. It measures 10 feet (3.2 m) long and weighs less than 1 ton (1 tonne). It might be the lightweight among rhinos, but the Sumatran is still far larger than most mammals. The other three types of rhino fall somewhere between these two in terms of size and weight. Female rhinos are usually about the same size as the males or a little smaller.

Horned Beasts

The word *rhinoceros* means "horn-nosed." All rhinos have at least one horn, even the babies. Indian and Javan rhinos have just one horn on top of their snout. White, black, and Sumatran rhinos have two horns. The larger horn is always the one closer to the front of the snout.

Rhinos use their horns to fight other rhinos and to defend themselves against enemies. With its head lowered and its foot pawing the ground ready to charge, an angry rhino is an extremely scary sight. Most **predators** that approach with the idea of attacking a rhino think again upon seeing this fearsome animal ready to fight.

The largest land mammal ever to inhabit Earth was an early type of rhino. It lived about 35 million years ago. It stood 15 feet (4.6 m) at the shoulder. Unlike modern rhinos, this ancient rhino didn't have horns.

13

Black rhinos (right) and white rhinos shared a common ancestor about five million years ago before gradually developing into two different species.

Hairy Horns

A rhinoceros's horns are made of **keratin**— the same material as hair. The horn is actually a mass of hairlike fibers clumped together. Hooves, feathers, beaks, and fingernails are all made of keratin, too.

Unlike the horns of cattle, the rhino's horn has no bony core. If a rhino's horn is broken off in a fight, there is hardly any blood. The broken horn will soon begin to grow back. The black rhino has the longest horn of any of the rhinos. Its larger horn can grow up to a whopping 4½ feet (1.4 m) long.

Armor Plating

In medieval times, knights wore suits of armor, made of overlapping metal plates. Rhinos look as if they are wearing armor, too! The thick skin of Indian, Javan, and Sumatran rhinos is pleated into deep folds that resemble a suit of armor. Knobby bumps on the rhino's skin resemble metal **rivets**, completing the armor-plated look. Though still pleated, the African rhinos have smoother skin.

At first glance, most rhinos appear to be almost hairless. But in fact, they have hair all over their body. Some Sumatran rhinos are covered with coarse, or rough, hair. In other species, the most noticeable hairs are on the eyelashes, ears, and particularly the tail. The rhinos use their tail as a fly swatter to keep pesky insects from biting them.

An Indian rhino has few visible hairs on its armorlike skin. The hairiest rhino was the woolly rhino, which died out about 10,000 years ago. It was covered in thick fur.

Black rhinos are also called hook-lipped rhinos. As this black rhino enjoys a mud bath, its protruding upper lip is clearly visible.

A Coat of Mud

A rhino's skin can be almost an inch (2.5 cm) thick in places. However, the top layer of skin is thin and sensitive. Insects can easily puncture it, or it can get sunburned.

To protect their sensitive skin, rhinos cover themselves in mud or spend time in the water. Indian rhinos lounge around in water holes. African rhinos roll in shallow, muddy pools called **wallows**, until they are covered in mud from head to foot. When the mud dries it forms a protective coat, which protects the rhino from the harsh sunlight.

All rhinos have gray skin, even white and black rhinos. However, rhinos tend to look like the color of the mud in which they roll.

Feet and Tracks

Rhinos have sturdy legs to support their giant bulk. Each foot has three broad toes. Each toe is protected by a strong, blunt nail, which is actually a kind of hoof.

When walking, most of the rhino's weight is supported by the middle toe. This toe is wider than the other two toes. The rhino leaves a footprint that resembles the ace of clubs in a pack of playing cards. These prints are very easy to identify. Experts tracking rhinos across the African grasslands can easily tell where a rhino has been by its tracks, or footprints.

The soles of a rhino's feet are soft and elastic. That helps balance the animal's great weight.

A black rhino charges at an intruder. Black rhinos are known for being the most aggressive of all the rhinos.

Sporty Rhinos

As one of the world's heaviest animals, rhinos might be expected to be slow movers. In fact, they can run very quickly if necessary. A charging rhino can run at 30 miles (48 km) per hour for some distance. As well as being fast, these beasts are also quite agile. A rhino can change direction at a moment's notice, and it can accelerate faster than a truck.

Rhinos spend a lot of time around water and are good swimmers. The Indian rhino is probably the best swimmer. It can cross wide rivers and dive underwater. Sumatran rhinos are also strong swimmers. These rhinos have been seen swimming in the ocean.

Sounds and Smells

Like humans, rhinos have five senses: sight, smell, hearing, taste, and touch. Their most developed senses are smell and hearing. Their leaf-shaped ears swivel back and forth to channel sounds into their inner ears. A rhino's long snout is filled with hollow chambers that gather scents floating in the air.

Humans rely mostly on eyesight. Rhinos, however, are nearsighted. Tests have shown that a rhino cannot tell the difference between a human and a small tree at a distance of about 100 feet (30 m)! The rhino's small eyes are located on the sides of its head. Rhinos, therefore, have a wide field of vision. However, there is also a downside to having eyes on the sides of the head. The rhino has to move its head to see what is right in front of its nose!

Eat Your Greens!

Rhinos are herbivores, or plant eaters. A rhino needs to eat a lot of greens every day just to keep going. Some species eat mainly grass, while others **browse** on leaves, shrubs, and even fruit. A rhino's lips and mouth are shaped to tackle the particular food it eats.

White rhinos **graze** on short grass. They have a special ridge inside their mouth that nips off stalks, and a wide mouth that is ideal for **cropping** grass. In fact, some people think that the white rhino was originally named the "wide rhino" for the shape of its mouth. The other species of rhinos have a pointed mouth with flexible lips. The lips are ideal for stripping leaves off branches and even for plucking small fruit.

The thick layer of dried mud protects this white rhino's skin from sunburn and also acts as a barrier against biting insects.

Crush and Stab!

Grass and leaves are tough and need to be chewed thoroughly. Rhinos have broad, flat teeth, called **molars**, at the back of their jaws. These teeth are ideal for grinding plants. African rhinos do not have any front teeth. However, like other rhinos, African rhinos do have a stomach with several chambers that helps to break down tough, stringy plants.

Asian rhinos have pointed teeth called **incisors** in the front of their jaws. These teeth are mainly used as weapons, not for crunching on plants. Rather than using their horns when fighting, Asian rhinos jab at enemies with their lower front teeth.

Black rhinos graze and browse on more than 200 different types of plants.

29

Oxpeckers pick insects off rhinos, zebras, domestic cattle, giraffes, and buffalo.

The Odd Couple

A rhino spends its life in the company of a bird called an oxpecker. This odd couple forms a kind of partnership, which both animals find useful. It is rare to see a rhino without one or more of these feathered friends.

The oxpecker rides around on the rhino's back and hops all over its body. It picks off fleas and ticks that have attached themselves to the mammal's skin. The bird gets a meal, and the rhino gets rid of pesky **parasites**. The bird also feeds on insects stirred up from the ground by the rhino's hooves. Both animals are also safer when together. The wary oxpecker is safe from its enemies by perching on the big mammal's back. In return, the bird warns the rhino of strangers approaching.

Day and Night

Rhinos may be active during the day or night, depending on where they live. On the plains of Africa, it's too hot to stand in the sun feeding during the day. Therefore, African rhinos spend the day under a shady tree or in a muddy pool. In the late afternoon, they venture into the sun as they head for their favorite feeding spots. They browse or graze in the cool of the night. Young rhinos may spend the night chasing one another and splashing about in water holes.

Asian rhinos can be more active by day because they live in cool, shady forests. Even so, they often take time out for a nap between daytime feedings.

White rhinos spend
about 12 hours each
day grazing.

White rhinos mingle
peacefully in small
groups as they graze.

34

Sometimes Sociable

Most types of rhinos are solitary—they live alone—with the exception of mothers and their young. Black rhinos are loners with a reputation for being bad-tempered and unpredictable.

White rhinos are a little more sociable. They spend time in groups of up to 18 animals. These groups are made up of one male and several females and their young. White rhinos are more easygoing than black rhinos. However, a mother will attack any intruder that comes between her and her young.

Indian rhinoceroses also like company. Sometimes, several of these rhinos share the same muddy wallow.

Home Sweet Home

Every rhino has its own **territory**—an area where it feeds and rests. If food and water are plentiful, the territory is small. If they are scarce, each rhino needs a bigger space in which to find enough food.

The territory of a **bull**, or male, rhino is usually smaller than that of a female, or **cow**. Males fiercely defend their territory. They mark the borders of their territory with droppings. They do not allow other males in their claimed area. Indian rhinos leave piles of dung up to 3 feet (1 m) high at the edges of their territory!

The cows are less bothered by other females entering their territory. The territory of female white rhinos often overlap. When these cows meet, they greet each other nose to nose.

The size of a rhino's territory varies from 1 to 6 square miles (3 to 15 sq km).

White rhino bulls fight.
One bull has hooked its
horn under its rival's leg
in an attempt to topple it.

38

Getting Together

Even rhinos that are solitary by nature get together to **mate**. A cow that is ready to mate will go wandering. As she passes through the territories of several bulls, she gives off a scent. The scent tells the males that she is ready to mate.

If more than one bull picks up her scent, there might be a fight. The bulls square up, wiping their horns on the ground and spraying smelly urine. If neither backs down, they might charge at each another. Rhinos have been killed after being gored by their rival's teeth or horns.

Males and females do not always get along. The courting couple might charge at each other with heads lowered! Eventually, they make peace and mate. The male usually sticks around for a few days afterward. But in the end, he wanders off, and the female is left to raise her young alone.

Giving Birth

Baby rhinos spend a long time developing inside their mother. The time between mating and birth is called **gestation**. Rhinos have a longer gestation period than most mammals—about 15 months. Cows usually give birth to just one young, called a **calf**, but occasionally twins are born.

A newborn rhino is tiny compared to its mother. However, compared to most mammal babies, baby rhinos are enormous! A newborn black rhino weighs about 88 pounds (40 kg) and is about 2 feet (60 cm) tall. The calf looks like a miniature version of its mother, and it even has a tiny horn.

A six-week-old white rhino calf drinks its mother's milk as she has a drink from a river.

A young white rhino stays close to its mother—not only for milk but also for protection.

First Foods

Young hoofed mammals are usually on their feet shortly after birth. A rhino calf is up and taking its first wobbly steps within hours of being born.

Within a few days, the baby is trotting along beside its mother as she wanders in search of food. Like all young mammals, the calf knows to drink its mother's milk. A young rhino drinks a lot of milk—about 50 pints (23 l) every day. Just a few weeks after birth, the baby is sampling its first taste of leaves or grass. But the calf continues to drink its mother's milk throughout its first year.

Predators Beware!

An adult rhino is so big that even the fiercest predators, such as lions and tigers, will not attack it. However, rhino calves are at risk not just from big cats, but also from packs of hyenas and sharp-toothed crocodiles that lurk in water holes.

A female rhino is a careful mother. She keeps a watchful eye on her calf and calls it close at the first sign of danger. White rhinos sometimes form a defensive ring, facing outward with their calves in the center if danger threatens. Few predators are bold or foolish enough to tackle a wall of angry rhinos!

A white rhino calf takes a break after playing.

45

With luck, this young black rhino might live to 40 years.

Growing Up

At about one month old, the calf is getting stronger by the day—and looking for fun! If it grows up in the company of other calves, the youngsters play together. They chase one another in games of tag and have pushing contests. If there are no calves to play with, the mother must make do as a playmate. The baby charges her or tries to sneak up on her from behind.

The youngster sticks close to its mother until it is about three years old. It's then time to set up its own territory, as its mother prepares to give birth again. Rhinos start to have babies of their own between five and eight years old. They reproduce slowly, only giving birth once every four or five years. That is one of the reasons why rhinos are rare.

Protecting Rhinos

Rhinos are among the world's rarest animals. Experts believe that there are only about 20,000 rhinos left in the wild. Asian rhinos are particularly rare. Scientists think there are only about 60 Javan rhinos left. Unfortunately, this species is in danger of **extinction**.

A few centuries ago, rhinos were much more common. But many have been killed by humans for meat and also for their horns. Some people use the ground-up horns in traditional medicines. The habitats where rhinos live are also disappearing, as people build new towns, roads, and farms.

Luckily, **reserves** and parks have been set up in parts of Africa and Asia. Most rhinos now live in these protected places, where they are safe from harm. With careful management, rhinos will continue to wander the forests and splash in water holes for many centuries to come.

Words to Know

Browse   To feed on leaves or shrubs.

Bull   A male rhinoceros.

Calf   A young rhinoceros.

Cow   A female rhinoceros.

Cropping   Cutting short.

Extinction   When all the animals in a species die out and are gone forever.

Gestation   The period of time when a young animal develops inside its mother.

Graze   To eat grass.

Incisors   The teeth at the front of the jaws.

Keratin   The tough material that makes up a rhino's horns and hooves.

Mammal	Any animal with hair or fur that feeds its young on milk.
Mate	To come together to produce young.
Molars	Broad back teeth used for grinding.
Parasites	Small animals that live on or in other animals and feed on their body tissues.
Predators	Animals that hunt others animals.
Reserves	Protected areas where harming animals is forbidden by law.
Rivets	Metal pins or bolts with a head.
Species	The scientific word for animals of the same type that breed together.
Territory	An area that an animal defends as its own private space.
Wallow	A shallow pool where rhinos cool off.

Find Out More

Books

Carson, M. K. *Emi and the Rhino Scientist*. Scientists in the Field. Boston, Massachusetts: Houghton Mifflin, 2007.

Orme, H. *Rhinos in Danger*. Wildlife Survival. New York: Bearport Publishing, 2006.

Web sites

Creature Feature: Black Rhinoceroses
kids.nationalgeographic.com/Animals/CreatureFeature/Black-rhinoceros
Information and pictures of black rhinos.

Rhinoceros
www.enchantedlearning.com/subjects/mammals/rhino/Rhinoprintout.shtml
Facts about rhinos and a picture of a white rhino to print and color in.

Index